PENGUIN BOOKS

THE *WOMAN'S DAY*® BOOK OF
CHILDREN'S BIRTHDAY PARTIES

Frances Zweifel was born in Virginia, but the U.S. Air
Corps/Air Force moved the family nearly every year. She
has lived on air force bases around the country, on a
farm, in a small town, and in a large city. She attended
six grade schools and four different high schools. This
provided opportunities for meeting people from all across
the United States—and for learning regional twists to
birthday parties. (With four siblings and an energetic
mother, the parties were numerous.)

Mrs. Zweifel has been a biological illustrator since
1956. She and her scientist husband reared their three
children in New Jersey, where she also taught art and
music. She continues to illustrate for scientists, and has
written and/or illustrated several children's books. She
intends to go on doing this well into the future, from her
home base in the mountains of eastern Arizona.

The
Woman's Day®
Book of Children's Birthday Parties

*Do-It-Yourself Parties
for All Seasons*

Frances Zweifel

PENGUIN BOOKS

PENGUIN BOOKS
Published by the Penguin Group
Viking Penguin, a division of Penguin Books USA Inc.,
375 Hudson Street, New York, New York 10014, U.S.A.
Penguin Books Ltd, 27 Wrights Lane,
London W8 5TZ, England
Penguin Books Australia Ltd, Ringwood,
Victoria, Australia
Penguin Books Canada Ltd, 2801 John Street,
Markham, Ontario, Canada L3R 1B4
Penguin Books (N.Z.) Ltd, 182–190 Wairau Road, Auckland 10, New Zealand

Penguin Books Ltd, Registered Offices:
Harmondsworth, Middlesex, England

First published in Penguin Books 1991

1 3 5 7 9 10 8 6 4 2

LIBRARY OF CONGRESS CATALOGING IN PUBLICATION DATA
Zweifel, Frances W.
The *Woman's Day®* book of children's birthday parties : do-it-
yourself parties for all seasons / Frances Zweifel.
p. cm.
Includes index.
ISBN 0 14 01.0372 4
1. Children's parties. 2. Birthdays. I. Woman's Day®.
II. Title. III. Title: Book of children's birthday parties.
GV1205.Z89 1991
793.2′1—dc20   90-45931

Printed in the United States of America

For all children who have birthdays this year—
with love, Frances Zweifel

I want to acknowledge with gratitude the long-suffering patience and support of my writers' group: Margaret Cooper, Constance DeMott, and Miriam Rinn. Heartfelt thanks go also to my editor, Deborah Brodie, whose faith in me and this book never wavered, and who deserves a medal for perseverance.

Contents

Order Out of Chaos

Remember how it was when you were young? A birthday was a day of days, yours alone, and the party an occasion where you were the star.

It was not just another party: it was yours, with your friends to celebrate your day. When the cake came in, ablaze with candles, everyone stood by while you made your wish and strained to blow out all the little flames at once.

Today, the parties you stage will mark great days—and establish treasured memories—for both you and your children. They can be elaborate. They can be simple. There's just one guideline you must observe. Rule One: Plan the party so it's a pleasure for you to give, as well as a pleasure for the birthday child.

When your child can help with party preparations, you stretch the child's pleasure. There is the anticipation beforehand. And when the great day arrives, the child can say, "I did it!"

Just keep Rule One in mind. If you must ration the time you give to the party preparation, don't feel you must use all the party ideas in the book. Decide on those you can handle, bypass the others. And even if you're a natural-born party-giver, capable of doing everything, keep in mind your child's capacities, too. You may need to pick and choose among the party ideas to focus on the makeables that suit your child's attention span and talents.

If you and your child have fun planning the party, you both will have a better time, and fonder memories of the occasion.

Party Plans

This book offers plans for two parties for each season of the year, one indoors, one outdoors. Each plan includes directions for making invitations, decorations, favors, and food. There is also a complete program of games for each party.

All the plans are simple enough for you and your child to work out together. The materials required are household items, or inexpensive to purchase and readily available.

So turn to your birthday season, and the two special parties planned for it. Of course, if you and your child prefer a party from a different season, borrow the ideas from that one.

Party Strategy

Even the best-behaved children can be excitable and hard to manage in a large group in a small home. Think about having an additional adult or teenager to help you.

Prudent party-givers also remove valuable and fragile items from the party space, or anything that may be dangerous for a child to handle. Excited children can't be expected to take notice of such possessions.

For an indoor party, invite about the same number of guests as the birthday child's age.

For a larger group, such as your child's entire class, it may be best to hold the party outdoors, where some team and circle games can be played with more freedom and less damage. If a backyard is not available, you might move your party to a nearby park.

If your outdoor party is rained out, just transfer most of these parties inside by switching to quieter games. Or make running games less rambunctious by clearing the floor and having the children do their racing on hands and knees. (Several days before the event, you might leaf through the book for alternate game ideas, just in case.)

Most indoor parties can be held outdoors (except the Haunted House Party, and the Art Party if the day is windy). Just move the decorations and add an active game or two.

Party Booty

Every successful birthday party includes favors for the guests to take home. The favors suggested in this book tie in with the party themes, and some are used in the games, or as decorative elements. If several favors are to be carried home, provide paper bags for the departing guests.

Balloons are a must for these parties, as decorations, game equipment, and extra favors.

Prizes are not absolutely necessary, of course, but game winners love the recognition. You can make fancy "medals," as in the Snowflake Party and the Space Party. If you buy the prizes, try to find small items that carry out the party's theme.

Some parents think that birthday presents are enough loot

for the birthday child, and that he should not receive any prizes, even if he wins a game. If that's your rule, be quite sure your child understands it well before the party begins.

When should birthday presents be opened? Your answer is probably dictated by what's customary in your neighborhood. The birthday child is surely eager to know what delights are in the packages, and the givers equally eager to see how he reacts to their gifts. But remember that if presents are opened at the start of the party, your guests may want to play with them rather than join in the games you've planned. After lunch or just before the guests go home may be a better time for the opening.

The Food

Birthday parties are enough excitement for children, so it's best not to ask them to try new ideas in eating.

Refreshments can be plain, relying mainly on such familiars as hot dogs, peanut butter, simple variations on pizzas and hamburgers. The wise adult provides nothing that can be thrown like a ball!

Some children refuse to eat birthday cakes—they just want to admire such creations and blow out the candles. But almost everybody eats ice cream.

Much of the food suggested in these plans you can buy ready-to-eat, if you're on a schedule that makes last-minute food preparation impossible, and most require minimum cooking time, few dishes, and uncomplicated serving and cleanup.

When It's Time to Calm Down

Many children simmer down when refreshments are served. But any time the level of excitement reaches your highest tolerance, calm the children by singing a song together or reading a story to them. Several days before the party, search the library or bookstore for two or three illustrated books on the party's theme.

If your party includes music, with or without singing, consider borrowing tapes or records from the library or from friends. (You can't depend on radio for something appropriate.)

The parties in this book will last from two to three hours. To shorten the time, just eliminate a game. To lengthen the party, add a game from another party plan. Switch the games around to suit yourself.

Are Siblings Welcome?

An uninvited younger or older sibling may feel left out of the gang. If the brother or sister is allowed to help—*really* help, as in carrying cups, serving snacks, collecting and folding gift wrap—there will be fewer hurt feelings. This child should have a party favor, and perhaps a badge with "Helper" printed on it. (A little recognition smooths a lot of ruffled feathers.)

If the older child would rather go somewhere else, to play with other children, you may be wise to accept that solution. As for toddlers or babies, they will be much happier elsewhere during an older sibling's party.

Too Old or Too Young for the Games?

Some parties, such as the Animal Fair Party and the Art Party, are suited to younger or more quiet groups. You can adapt any party for a younger or older group, however, by switching or adding games from another party.

Rule One, Again

Sharing party preparations with your child can provide pleasurable times together. But if your time is limited, and a do-together project looks like just one more impossible hurdle, eliminate what you can't handle. Ignore that project, or buy a simple replacement. (But remember that shopping also takes time.)

Simple recipes for the refreshments are provided in this book. There is no law insisting that you must bake a birthday cake from scratch. Cake made from a mix will taste just fine. You can even use a plain bought cake for any party plans in this book.

Many of the ideas for these eight birthday parties came from my own childhood. Our mother was the most inventive party-giver I ever knew; we five children enjoyed some wildly funny parties—and some pretty weird ones, too! Other ideas were contributed by children, their parents, and their grandparents, from all across the United States, from Canada, and from Australia.

Circle and guessing games haven't changed very much. Children still enjoy the ones played at parties years ago, although the games may go by different names today.

When you and your child decide which birthday party you want, you should add or subtract whatever you like. Allow plenty of time for enjoying the preparations, take it easy—and have fun!

Key to Symbols

Adult help will be needed

Adult and child activity

Indoor party

Outdoor party

For younger children (4, 5, 6)

For older children (7, 8, 9)

Birthday Party Invitations

Basic Invitation

Use almost any kind of paper—typing bond, colored construction paper, or cut-up paper bags.

This basic invitation fits into an ordinary small business envelope, 3½ by 6½ inches. You can vary the invitation by drawing different designs or by cutting the card into a shape that fits a particular party theme.

Cut the paper to make a 6¼ inch square. Fold it in half.

The outside page tells the birthday child's name and the theme of the party: *Matt's Haunted House Party*. A design or picture announces the party's theme (directions are given with each party plan).

Inside the invitation, give all the necessary information about the party:

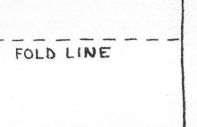

A Spooky Supper
at Matt Karlson's
319 Owl Creek Road

Oct. 23, 5 to 8 o'clock
Call Matt at 623-4118
Please arrive
EXACTLY at 5 P.M.!

Place (address)
Date
Time
Special instructions (suggestions about what to wear, or
   things to bring to the party; such details are given with
   each party plan)

If you are serving lunch or supper, be sure to say so on
the invitation.

At the bottom of the page, give the birthday child's tele-
phone number and ask the invited guests to let you know
whether they can come. (If they don't call back, call them—
so you will know how many to expect.)

Winter

Is there anything more exciting than being an astronaut? Boys and girls are enthralled with the exploits of men and women in space. So here's a party built around their fantasies.

"Space" is easy to conjure up with decorations: Balloons in blue, red, and yellow brighten the room for this winter party, and these colors, accented with gold and silver, carry over into the table settings.

You might let your young adventurers make their own Space Age Sundaes as the final treat.

Theme

Planets, stars, comets, moon, and sun; spaceships and astronauts; aliens from outer space.

Invitations

See Basic Invitation, page xix. Use light blue paper and a black crayon or felt-tip marker. In the center of the first page, print the birthday child's name and the party theme: *Dean's Space Party*. Paste gold or silver stars, bought at a stationery store, around the words.

Decorations

Cut out stars, comets, planets, the moon, and the sun from bright yellow poster board. Cover some with kitchen foil to make them silver. Tape them around the party room, to drapes and door frames, or hang them from light fixtures and curtain rods. If you have posters with a space theme, hang them, too. Use lots of balloons for color, tying them to chairs, curtain rods, stair railings.

A blue tablecloth and red or white plates and cups carry out the theme. If you use paper plates, paste gold and silver stars on the plate rims and the sides of the cups.

Cut out big silver stars from heavy-duty kitchen foil and place them down the middle of the table.

You can make a rocket-model centerpiece, with three different sizes of cardboard tubes, tape, and paint. Use toilet tissue and paper-towel tubes, and perhaps tall, narrow cans that once held potato chips or cookies. 1. Stuff the largest tube with crumpled paper. 2. Push the middle-sized tube down into the crumpled paper, and tape it firmly to the larger tube to prevent wobbling. 3. Stuff some crumpled paper into the middle tube. 4. Push the smallest tube into the open end of the middle tube, and tape it firmly in position. 5. Cut out a circle of construction paper about 4 inches in diameter (trace around a cup or funnel to draw the circle). Cut a slit to the center of the paper circle, cut out a quarter-circle wedge, and slide the cut edges over each other to form a pointed cone. Tape the cone closed. **6.** Now tape the cone over the open end of the smallest tube. **7.** You can cover the rocket completely with kitchen foil, or paint it silver or any color with poster paints. Allow time for the paint to dry before the party. **8.** Tape the completed rocket to a flat base—use cardboard or a wooden cutting board covered with colored paper.

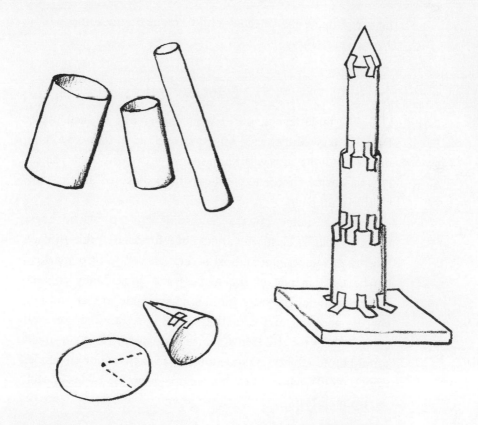

For the front door, cut a comet with a big tail from bright yellow poster board. Use red felt-tip marker or paint to print

the party theme and birthday child's name on the comet's tail: *Dean's Space Party*.

Favors

For table favors, put a white paper cup at each place. Print "Mars Munchies" on each cup with red crayon or marker. Fill the cups with such snacks as dried apricots, dates, raisins, coated chocolate candies, cheese-flavored snacks, and bubble-gum balls.

For take-home favors, buy some zip-top plastic bags, or small manila clasp envelopes, one for each child. In each bag or envelope, put a box of crayons or felt-tip markers (to be used in one of the games) and some fancy stickers from the stationery store (gold stickers come in star and sun shapes, and you may also find other interesting shapes and colors). Print the children's names and "Space Log" on small, spiral-bound tablets. Include a tablet in each bag or envelope. Print a child's name on each envelope or on the tablet in each see-through bag.

Food

- Milky Way Juice (milk or cocoa)
- Chicken & Stars soup (from cans)

- UFOs (small pita breads, split open and filled with shredded cheddar cheese and crisp bacon slices, put back together and heated until the cheese melts; OR slices of bread cut into circles to make grilled cheese sandwiches with crisp bacon inside)
- Orange slices (peeled oranges, sliced into rounds)
- Birthday cake (loaf-shaped plain cake, such as pound cake, frosted lightly with any favorite frosting and sprinkled with silver dragées for stars; arrange yellow or white candles in a crescent moon)
- Outer Space Sundaes (one or two scoops of vanilla ice cream on a thin slice of birthday cake. Offer a tray with bowls of various toppings, such as chocolate and butterscotch sauce, chocolate sprinkles, cherries, tiny marshmallows; place a serving spoon in each bowl)

Games

Some games will have winners. To make medals for prizes, you need:

poster board (gold, silver, or light blue)
blue ribbon, ½ to 1 inch wide,
   about 6 inches for each medal
large safety pins
scissors (use blunt safety scissors for young children)
a stapler

Count the games and the number of possible winners to be sure you make enough medals, and add a few extras to be safe. 1. Cut out stars from the poster board (you can use a cookie cutter to trace the stars). 2. Cut the ribbon into pieces 6 inches long. 3. Fold each ribbon in half and staple the ends

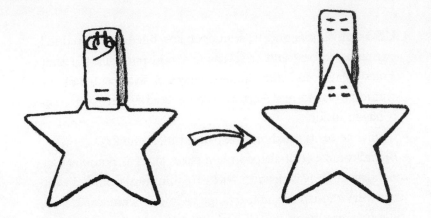

to the back of a star. **4.** Staple the upper bar of a large safety pin to the back of the ribbon, near the fold.

Simple put-together glider kits, bought from the variety store, would also be good prizes.

RACE TO THE MOON. For two players at a time. **1.** Make two paper cones, using lightweight paper. For each cone, cut an 8-inch circle from letter paper (trace around a plate to draw the circle). Cut to the center of the circle in one place. Slide the cut edges over each other until a cone is formed, and tape to secure the cone shape. There should be a tiny opening at the point of the cone, or snip one with scissors.

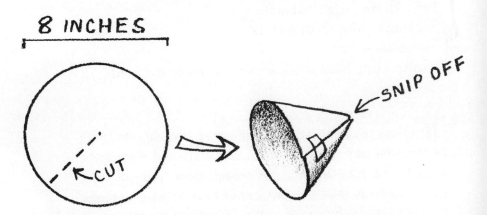

8 INCHES

CUT

SNIP OFF

2. String each cone on a length of strong thread about 10 feet long (use buttonhole thread or fine fishing line). **3.** Stand two chairs back to back, about 8 feet apart. **4.** Tie one end of each string to the back of one chair and the other ends of the strings to the second chair. Move the chairs apart so the strings are tight. The paper cones should slide easily along the strings.

Pull both cones to one chair, their open ends toward the chair back. Tape a picture of Planet Earth on this chair, or a card with "Earth" printed on it. Tape a picture of the moon or the word "Moon" to the second chair.

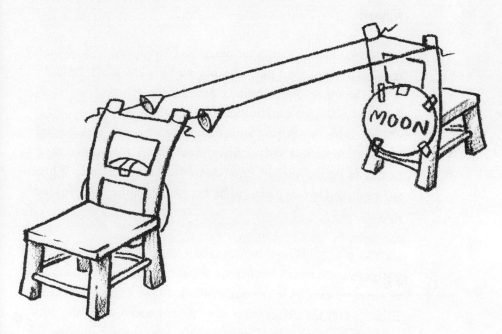

A player stands behind each cone. At a signal, they begin to blow into the cones. As the players puff and blow, the cones will move along the threads toward the Moon chair. The first child whose cone reaches the Moon is the winner.

If all this puffing and blowing seems too difficult, you can shorten the distance between Earth and Moon. Give each win-

ner a prize—or they can have a play-off until there is only one winner.

BLINDFOLD BLAST-OFF. One player is blindfolded. The others make a circle around her. She begins to count down from 10 while the others move quietly around the room. ". . . 3, 2, 1—Blast off!" the blindfolded player calls.

The others must stop where they are while the blindfolded player tries to find and identify them. They may move their bodies to dodge her but must keep both feet in place. When she finds and names a player, he becomes the next blindfolded player.

LOST IN SPACE. With a rope, make a large circle in the middle of the room, at least 8 feet across or larger. Scatter some peanuts or wrapped candies in the circle, about 10 pieces for each child. Blindfold all the players and have them kneel around the outside of the circle. At a signal, they crawl into the circle to search for the "lost" goodies. They may keep those they find.

AROUND-THE-MOON RELAYS. There must be an even number of players for this team game. The players form two lines. Set up a base at the far end of the room, such as a chair or box (you can tape a picture of the moon on this base).

Give each team a balloon and a paper or cardboard fan. The players must fan the balloons along the floor, around the base, and back to their teams.

Then the next player in line takes the fan and does the same. The first team to finish wins.

ALIENS. It may be helpful to show a finished example to the children before they begin this game—see the illustration on page 12.

The children sit or stand around a table, or they may sit on the uncarpeted floor. You need as many large sheets of drawing paper as there are children.

Fold each sheet into three parts and then unfold. Give a sheet of paper to each child. Using crayons from the bags of favors, each child draws the head and neck of a weird creature on the top section. The neck must stop just at the first fold. Now fold the top section to the back of the paper, and pass the paper to the player on the right.

The second player must draw the middle of the alien's body, beginning at the neck marks on the fold of the drawing but *not* looking to see the head part. He ends this middle section at the second fold line, marking it so the next player can see where to begin. He folds the middle drawing to the back of the paper, and passes the paper to the player on his right.

This third player now draws the bottom of the creature—legs, tentacles, whatever she wants—again without looking to see what is folded to the back. When all three parts have been drawn, unfold the drawings to see what the aliens look like.

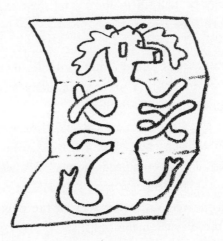

THE BLACK HOLE. This calls for a record or tape player, or a bell, an adult party helper to play the music, and a sheet of paper about 12 inches square for each player (have some extra sheets on hand in case some tear during the game). The sheets are all white, except one which is black, or has a big black circle drawn on it. This is the Black Hole. Draw a star on each white sheet of paper. Tape all the papers down in a large circle on the floor (test to see that they won't slip).

Each player stands on a sheet of paper. Now the party helper begins to play music (or rings the bell), and the players march around the circle, stepping from one paper to the next. Suddenly the music stops—and whoever is standing on the Black Hole at that moment must leave the game. He takes one star paper with him.

The music starts again, and stops again, and another person is caught in the Black Hole. Each time the Black Hole catches a player, there are fewer players. (You may have to retape the remaining papers to make a smaller circle.) Finally, only one player is left: the winner.

After lunch and the birthday cake, the children may have enough time to play "Astronaut Says" (just like "Simon Says"), or listen to a story. They may take home their Mars Munchies, their bags or envelopes of favors, an alien picture, and a balloon.

Active games make this an ideal backyard event, with everyone in snowsuits or other cold-weather gear until it's time to go inside and eat. The party warms up with a sock jump and a race, and after two more lively games, it's time for food.

If you have snow on the ground, nature has already done most of your decorating for you. If not, create a winter snow scene with some sparkly decorations, indoors or outdoors.

In case of bad weather, you can move two of the games indoors, and substitute quiet games from other parties for the Sock Jump and the race.

Invitations

 See Basic Invitation, page xix. Use light blue paper, folded vertically. For each invitation, cut out a 3-inch circle

from white typing paper, and fold it as shown below. Cut out a snowflake design; unfold the circle. Paste a snowflake on each invitation, and beneath it print the birthday child's name and the party theme: *Karissa's Snowflake Party.*

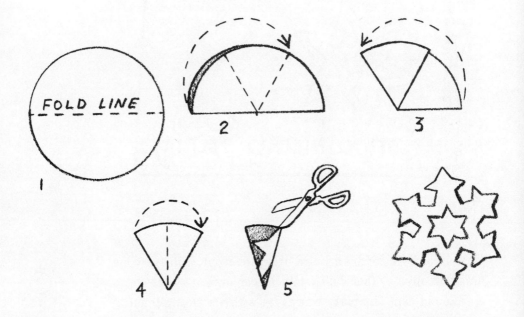

If the party will be outdoors, the invitation should say: Wear warm clothes (and boots, if necessary) for playing outdoors.

Decorations

The party colors should be wintry—light blue, white, and silver, with red accents.

Using ordinary white typing paper, cut out lots of snowflakes of different sizes (see the illustration above). Hang some snowflakes over the ends of twigs on bushes and trees, and tie others to branches with string. (A light wind won't do too much damage during the party period.) Inside, tie or tape your snowflakes everywhere you can reach.

Cut out one huge snowflake for the front door, or use several smaller ones. If your door is painted white, make this snowflake from light blue or silver paper. (Foil is not advisable because it is difficult to unfold without tearing.)

Tape the snowflake to the front door. Print a sign to tape under the snowflake, with the birthday child's name and the party theme.

Use a blue tablecloth and white plates and cups on the party table, with a row of snowflakes down the center. Tie red, blue, and white balloons to the chairs.

Favors

Wintertime is bell time, and jingle-bell anklets or bracelets are fun for your guests to wear. The bells make a cheerful noise during the party, and will be used in one of the games. For each anklet you will need:

    5 jingle bells
    a piece of narrow elastic about 18 inches long, OR a piece
      of red ribbon about 24 inches long

You can buy jingle bells at a variety store. Try to find some that ring loudly enough to be heard outdoors. 1.String one bell

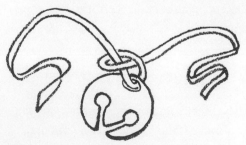

to the middle of the elastic, and knot the elastic to hold it in place. **2.** String and knot two more bells on both sides of the middle bell, about 1 inch apart. **3.** Tie the elastic around your birthday child's ankle, over his outdoor pants, and knot the ends. This size will probably fit your guests, too.

If you want to make bracelets, use a piece of elastic 10 inches long.

To make ribbon anklets or bracelets, string and tie the jingle bells this same way. Leave the ends of the ribbons long, and tie them on the children as they arrive at the party.

Food

- Hot Spiced Apple Juice (warm juice with a dash of cinnamon and cloves stirred in)
- Orange-Applesauce Gelatin (See recipe on page 94).
- Little Pizzas (You can fix these before the party and heat them when needed. See recipe on page 94.)
- Frosty Cupcakes (Use any flavor cupcakes, frosted with white icing. Draw a blue frosting snowflake on each cupcake, or just sprinkle them with blue sugar or silver dragées.) Place a birthday candle on each cupcake. At birthday cake time, group the cupcakes on a platter so the birthday child can blow out all the candles at once. Or each guest may want to blow out his own candle.
- Ice Cream Snowballs: Scoop round balls of ice cream, any flavor. Roll them in flaked coconut and return them to the freezer until serving time.

Games

Like the Olympic Winter Games, some of these party games have winners. For prizes, make fancy medals on ribbons.

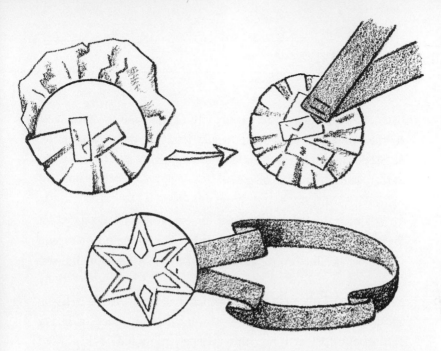

Count the games and number of possible winners to be sure you make enough medals, plus a few extras to be safe.

You can finish up the medals more easily if you and your child work assembly-line fashion, cutting out all the cardboard circles first, then all the ribbons, then the foil, and so on.

To make each medal, you will need:

blue ribbon, 1 inch wide and 24 inches long
thin cardboard
white paper
glue
scissors (sharp for cardboard, blunt safety for children)
a stapler
aluminum foil
tape

1. Cut out a 3-inch circle from the thin cardboard (you can trace the circle around a cup or tumbler). 2. Cut a piece of foil large enough to cover the circle front and back. 3. Press the foil firmly around the cardboard and tape it down on the

back. **4.** From the white paper, cut a snowflake the same size as the circle. **5.** Glue this on the front of the silver circle. **6.** Staple the crossed ends of the ribbon to the back of the medal; see illustration on page 19.

It's nice to provide a medal for everyone at the party, for favors. Make these with red ribbon. The game winners will then have two medals to wear, just like the Olympic medalists.

SOCK JUMP. This first game, which has no winner, is lively enough to warm up all the children. Take a piece of heavy cord about 15 feet long, and a knee-length red sock stuffed with rags, and tie the sock securely to the end of the cord.

The player chosen as Swinger stands in the middle of the yard, holding the free end of the cord. The rest of the players stand around her in a circle, just within reach of the sock at the end of the cord. Now the Swinger begins to swing the sock around the circle, at about ankle level. The other children must jump over the sock as it whirls by. Any player hit twice by the sock drops out of the game. The last player in the circle becomes the new Swinger.

ICE FLOE RACE.   Each player will need 2 pieces of cardboard big enough to stand on. Cut cardboards from empty cartons; one carton will provide 6 or more flat pieces. (**Caution:** *An adult should do this cutting.*) These cardboards are the "ice floes." The players will race from start to finish by stepping from one ice floe to the next.

The children line up on one side of the yard. At a signal, each player puts one piece of cardboard on the ground in front of him and steps on it. Then he puts the second cardboard down and steps to that. Now he must pick up the piece behind him and move it ahead, and then step to it.

Stepping from one ice floe to the next, the children race around a base at the other side of the yard (a bush or tree, or a chair set in the snow) and back to the starting line.

In very cold weather, you can play an even faster version of this game by working in pairs, one child moving the ice floes and the partner stepping. For pairs of racers, provide two medals, one for each of the two winners.

MUSICAL ICE FLOES. Make a row of the "ice floe" cardboards on the ground, using one fewer than the number of players. If there are more than six children, the ice floes can go in a double row.

The adult helper holds all the jingle-bell anklets while the players make a circle around the ice floes. Then the adult, who has a loud voice, shakes the jingle-bell anklets and begins singing "Jingle Bells" while the children march around and around the row of ice floes. Suddenly the music stops. The players must scramble to find an ice floe to sit on. Since there is one less ice floe than players, someone will not find a place. He leaves the game, taking an ice floe with him.

The singing and jingle bells start again; the music stops suddenly; and again each player must try to find an ice floe to sit on. Each time a player leaves the game, the circle of players and number of ice floes grow smaller. This goes on until there is only one player left: the winner.

FREEZE TAG. Choose a player to be "It." Set a limit on the playing area, such as the whole backyard, or part of it, one area of a playground, or the driveway.

At a signal, "It" runs after the other children and tries to tag someone. A tagged player must immediately "freeze," like a block of ice. She remains "frozen" until an untagged player runs by and touches her, "thawing" her to run again.

If "It" tags a second player before the first one can be "thawed," the second player tagged then becomes the new "It." This game will have no winners.

After these active games, everyone should be tired and hungry, and ready for lunch.

If there is time after the birthday cake, the children may like to sing "Jingle Bells," keeping time with their own jingle-bell anklets. Or they may play "I Looked in the Igloo" (a memory game played like "Pirate's Chest"; see page 43). The players begin each turn by saying, "I looked in the igloo and there I found . . . ," naming something to do with winter, ice, and snow (such as a penguin, an icicle, a warm coat).

The children may take home their jingle-bell anklets or bracelets, Olympic medals, and a balloon.

SPRING

Children who enjoy crafts will love this party. It features toys they can make for themselves, some art activities, and an amusing relay race. You can handle it alone with a small party group; if you have a large one, think about lining up a helper.

You'll want to roll up the rug in the room you use for the children's art projects. The party will work outdoors if the weather is warm but not windy.

Theme

Art and crafts, in a riot of color. Use lots of bright balloons—red, orange, purple, green, every color you can find.

Invitations

See Basic Invitation, page xix. Use any light-colored paper, such as yellow or orange. On the outside page, draw the outline of an artist's paint palette. Inside this palette, print the birthday child's name and the party theme: *Mollie's Art Party*. With colored markers or crayons, create spots of different colors around the edge of the palette.

Ask each guest to bring a smock or an old, long-sleeved shirt, adult size. (Have a few extras on hand for children who forget to bring their own.)

Decorations

For the front door, draw a big artist's palette on a sheet of poster board or cardboard. Cut out the palette shape.

(**Caution:** *An adult should cut the cardboard*.) Paint blobs of different colors around the edge of the palette, and print the birthday child's name and the party theme in the middle, as for the invitation. Tape or tack the palette to your front door.

Cover the party table with one big sheet of plain white or light-colored paper. Use colorful plates and cups. To make balloons stick to the ceiling and walls, blow up the balloons, then rub them on a blanket or carpet and touch them to the wall. The balloons will cling like magic.

Favors

At each child's place at the table, put a box of crayons or felt-tip markers. Write a guest's name on each box. The plain tablecloth is for the children to draw on as much as they like before the food is served. (If you provide felt-tip markers as favors, place layers of newspaper or a sheet of plastic under the tablecloth so the markers won't stain the table.)

During the party the children will make other things to take home. Have on hand a large paper bag for each child to carry home his art projects.

Food

• Red or purple fruit juice
• Carrot sticks
• Spaghetti with Meatballs and Tomato Sauce (See recipe on page 95; or buy your favorite prepared brand.)
• Pink or green ice cream
• Cake with pink frosting, the top encircled with green gum-drops

Games

For this party, most of the games will be art projects. When the childen arrive, they should put on their smocks (or adult-size shirts worn backwards) before they join the fun. Up to 5 or 6 children can work on one kind of project at the same time. If there are more guests, it would be well to set up 2 tables in different parts of the room, with an adult at each table to help and to make sure there are enough art supplies to go around.

PLAY-DOUGH. The play-dough project should be the first on your party schedule, because it takes time to bake—and cool—the finished products. Plan to bake the creations while other activities are going on, and cool the baked products during lunch. If there is time after the last project, "Wish People," the children can color their play-dough creations then.

You will need:

play-dough, homemade or bought
cookie cutters
rolling pins
pencils, blunt knives, forks, and other small tools to make
    marks on the finished creations

Recipe for homemade play-dough (make this the day before the party):

1 cup regular table salt
2 cups flour, sifted
¾ cup water
¼ teaspoon cooking oil

1. Mix the salt and sifted flour in a large bowl. 2. Stir in the water gradually. 3. Mix in the oil. (Add a few drops of vegetable color if you wish, but plain dough is better if you want to paint it later on.) 4. With your hands, squeeze the dough in the bowl until it clings together. 5. Move the dough to a counter or table, and knead it until it is smooth and feels like clay. 6. Wrap the dough in plastic and store it in the refrigerator until the party.

This recipe makes enough play-dough for two children. Make more play-dough in batches this size; bigger batches are hard to handle.

Play-dough can be modeled like clay to create small animals and other figures; it can also be rolled flat and cut with cookie cutters. Sprinkle the table and rolling pin with a little sifted flour so the dough won't stick. Add bits of dough, in tiny balls and snakes, to make extra features on the sculptures. Use a pencil or fork to produce lines and little holes.

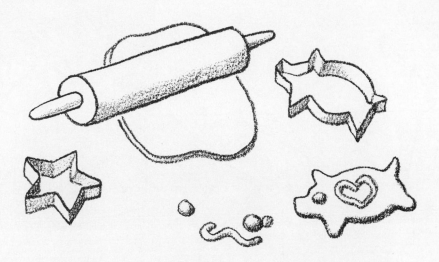

The figures can be baked in the oven while everyone moves on to the next project. Put them on a flat cookie sheet and bake at 300° F. for about an hour. Allow them to cool during lunch. Baked, cooled figures can be painted with poster paints or colored with felt-tip markers—at the party if time permits, or later on at home.

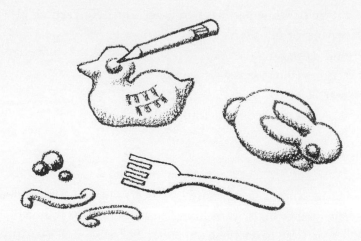

Although this play-dough is safe and nontoxic, it is not for eating.

PAPER-BAG PUPPETS. Look at the illustration above. Make up one puppet before the party, to give the children an idea of how to start. You will need:

> brown or white paper lunch bags, 2 or 3 for each child
> crayons or felt-tip markers
> colored paper
> scissors (blunt safety for young children)
> paste
> scraps of colored felt, cloth, ribbon, yarn
> tape
> a stapler

Suggest ideas to the children, such as big eyes, a flapping tongue, paper curls, yarn hair. Cut tongues from red or pink paper or felt; paste them in place. For hair, cut a strip of colored paper the width of the paper bag, snip one long edge into a "comb," and paste or staple it in place. Eyes can be created from buttons, cut-paper circles, or even the bottoms of paper cups. No doubt the children will have plenty of ideas of their own.

By putting their hands inside the bags, the children can make the puppets move their "heads." Write the children's names on their puppets.

DRESS-UP RELAY RACE. This is an active game, good to play after quiet crafts. You will need 2 bags of adult clothes, such as an old dress, pair of trousers, jacket, sweater, raincoat, long necklace, big hats, rain boots, shoes, gloves. There should be an even number of players. 1. The players form 2 teams at one end of the room. 2. Set a base, such as a chair, at the other end. 3. Give the first child on each team a bag of clothing. 4. At a signal, the 2 players must dress up in all the clothes in their bags, run to the base, take off the clothes, put the clothes back into the bags, and run back to their teams. 5. The next players in line do the same.

The first team to get all its players dressed and undressed wins. (Drawing tablets make good prizes.)

By this time the play-dough figures should have finished baking, and may be put on racks or towels to cool during lunch.

Before the food is served, the children may decorate the tablecloth with the crayons or markers they find at their places.

After the birthday cake, there is one more project to do.

WISH PEOPLE. You will need:

several rolls of strong paper such as heavy craft or wrapping paper (from stationery, art supply, or variety store); about 5 feet of paper for each child
scissors (blunt safety for young children)

crayons or markers (use the party favors)

tape

1. Spread a sheet of paper on the floor. 2. Have a child lie down on the paper, arms slightly out from her sides. 3. Draw the outline of the child on the paper. (If her arms don't fit, cut extra paper and tape to the edges.)

Now the children can color any costumes they desire— astronauts, dancers, whatever they wish they could be. The finished drawing can be cut out, if there is time. You may fasten a string at the top so the drawing can be hung up.

Before they go home, the children could put on a play with their paper-bag puppets. Read or tell a familiar story, substituting whatever characters the children have created. Or sing a favorite song together while the children move their puppets to "sing along." The children may take home their favors, their art projects, and a balloon.

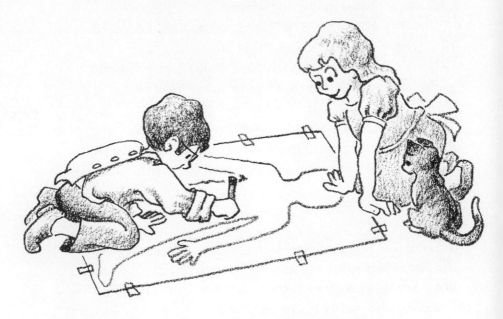

Here's a chance for everybody to dress up like a pirate, "walk the plank," hunt hidden treasure, play "pirate ships," and even find a buried surprise in the birthday cake.

The Pirate Ships game really needs outdoor space, and the Treasure Hunt is better if you have ample room. Otherwise the party can move indoors, with one substitute game.

Theme

Pirates, sailing ships, desert islands, treasure.

Invitations

See Basic Invitation, page xix. Use red paper, fold it, and turn it sideways. With a black crayon or marker, draw a Jolly

Roger (skull and crossed bones) along one edge of the first page. Beside this, print the birthday child's name and the party theme: *Ken's Pirate Party*.

Ask the guests to wear old clothes that fit in with the pirate theme, such as blue jeans or shorts, comfortable T-shirts, sneakers.

Decorations

Pirate colors are red, black, and white. To make a sign for your front door, you will need a sheet of white poster board, black and red poster paints, a pencil, and a brush. Draw a Jolly Roger flag on the poster board. Leaving the skull and bones white, paint the rest of the flag black. Below the flag, print the birthday child's name and the party theme, as on the invitation. Tape or tack the sign to the front door.

For the party table, use a red or white tablecloth. With a black construction paper place mat at each place, red or white plates and cups are appropriate. If you use paper cups, draw a black Jolly Roger on each.

Tie red and white balloons all around the party area, to chairs, fence, tree trunks. (If indoors, tie balloons to chairs, banisters, and curtain rods.)

Favors

As soon as the children arrive, give each one a red sash, a black eye patch, and one big golden earring. To make these, you will need:

red crepe paper (1 roll makes 6 sashes)
gold-colored curtain or drapery rings (1 ring for each child)
rubber bands

a square of black felt, about 8½ by 11 inches (available at
   variety or fabric stores)
thin black elastic (about 18 inches for each eye patch)
scissors (sharp for cutting felt and crepe paper)
a needle and black thread
a ruler

To make the sashes, cut the roll of crepe paper into 3 equal
parts. (**Caution:** *An adult should cut the crepe paper.*) Unfold
the 3 long strips, and cut each strip in half, to make 6 shorter
strips.

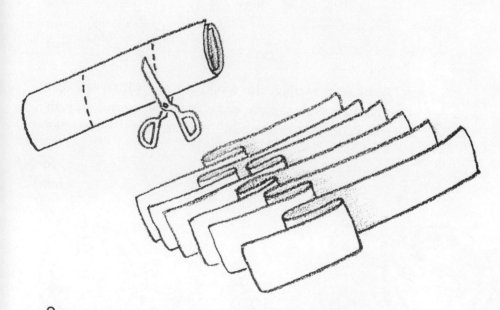

To make the eye patches: **1.** Cut pieces of black felt 2½
inches wide and 2 inches high. **2.** Cut the bottom of each patch
in a curve. **3.** Cut a piece of elastic about 18 inches long.
4. Sew the ends of the elastic to the upper corners of an eye
patch, and snip the elastic in the middle so there will be two

strings to tie in back of the wearer's head. Or snip two tiny slits in the upper corners of the eye patch, pass the elastic through the slits, and tie behind the head.

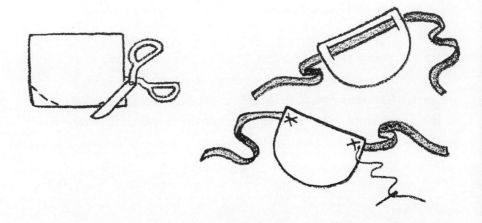

To make an earring, slip a rubber band halfway through a curtain ring. Now slip one end of the rubber band through the other end, and pull the inside loop up tight. To wear this

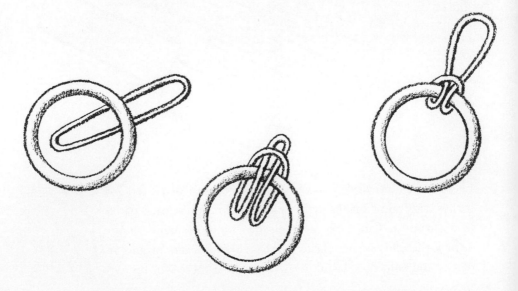

earring, stretch the rubber band loop over the ear. Make one earring for each guest. (Extra earrings would be good prizes. Game winners would then have two earrings to wear. Count the games with prize winners, to be sure you have enough earrings.)

A dagger to tuck into the sash is just the thing for this pirate outfit. Buy rubber daggers at a variety store, or cut play daggers out of heavy cardboard. (**Caution:** *An adult should do all the cutting.*) You will need:

cardboard sheets from grocery cartons
pencil
heavy knife or utility knife

1. On the cardboard, draw the outline of a dagger, about 7 or 8 inches long. Draw a simple design, easy to cut out. **2.** Cut out this dagger carefully, and use it as the design to draw more daggers on the cardboard. **3.** Cut out a dagger for each party guest.

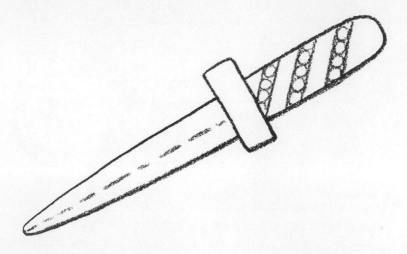

Food

- Buckets o' Blood (tomato soup in mugs)
- Desert Island Fruit Bowl (banana and orange slices)
- Pirate Patties (See recipe on page 96.)
- Ketchup
- Hard Tack (crackers or buttered biscuits)
- Ice cream
- Buried Treasure Cake

  To make cake, bake any flavor mix in a flat, single layer baking pan, 9 by 13 inches (or buy a sheet cake this size). When the cake has cooled completely, turn it over on a board or cookie sheet. With a thin-blade knife, cut off the corners and trim the cake in a more or less kidney-bean shape, to make an "island." Save the cutoff pieces. Cover a serving tray with blue paper or cloth; this will be the "ocean." Place the shaped cake on the "ocean." Now cut a small, square plug out of the cake, and set it aside. Wrap a small, flat "treasure," such as a 50-cent piece, in waxed paper or foil, and place this at the bottom of the plug hole. Pat the plug back into place in the cake, and *mark the spot with a toothpick.*

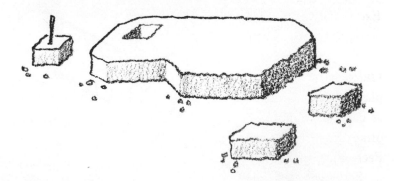

For ease in frosting, freeze the cake on its tray. Frost the cake with green icing, leaving the toothpick in place. Use the cut pieces of cake as rocks on the island; frost these with green or brown icing. Now write the birthday child's name on the cake: Ken's Treasure Island. You can add little trees (twigs with stems wrapped in foil). Note where the treasure is buried, and remove the toothpick.

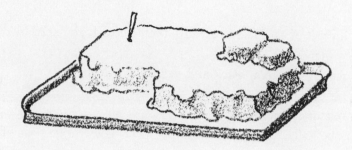

At birthday-cake time, give each child a toothpick with a numbered or named tag taped to it. After the candles have been blown out, the children stick their toothpicks where they guess the treasure is hidden. (**Hint:** Serve the treasure piece first, to forestall a messy search by the young guests.)

Games

Except for "Pirate Ships," all these games can be played indoors.

PIRATE SHIPS: One pirate stands in the middle of the yard or playground area. All the others stand in "coves," places such as corners, in front of a tree, or beside a bush. The middle pirate goes from cove to cove, asking for his ship to be let in. Each pirate in a cove sends him on to another.

Suddenly the pirate in the middle shouts, "All ships out!" All the other pirates must dash away from their own coves and try to get into another. While they are running, the pirate in the middle runs to one of the vacant coves. There will be a new pirate without a cove, and the game goes on. When the children tire of this, start the next game.

PIN THE PATCH ON THE PIRATE. This is a Pirate Party version of Pin the Tail on the Donkey. You will need:

a sheet of cardboard or white poster board, about 20 by 30 inches
felt-tip markers, black and yellow
black construction paper
scissors (blunt safety)
tape

1. On the cardboard, draw the face of a one-eyed pirate; draw the other eye closed. 2. Cut eye patches from the black paper,

one for each player. 3. Put a loop of tape on the back of each eye patch, sticky side out (or use double-faced tape).

Nail, tack, or tape the pirate picture to a tree, fence post, or perhaps a wall. Use strong tape outdoors, such as plastic or reinforced strapping tape; indoors, masking tape will do.

A blindfolded player holds a paper eye patch while someone turns him around three times. Then he heads toward the pirate picture and tries to stick his eye patch over the pirate's closed eye. He must use only one hand, and must leave the patch wherever it first touches. The player whose eye patch is closest to the pirate's closed eye is the winner.

WALKING THE PLANK. You will need a flat surface such as a driveway or sidewalk 20 feet or longer, and a long board. If you do not have a board, you can draw the "plank" with chalk; or use a long strip of paper such as paper towels or typing sheets taped together. The plank, whether board, chalk, or paper, should be about 6 inches wide.

Place the board down flat or draw the chalk "plank" on the driveway or sidewalk, or tape the paper down. The players line up at one end of the plank. Blindfold the first player. She must try to walk along the plank without stepping off into the "water" on either side.

If a foot steps off the plank, the other players shout "Water!" If both feet step off, the player has fallen into the water, and the next player takes a turn. The pirates who walk the plank without falling off could share a small bag of jelly beans or other tasty treat.

TREASURE HUNT. This project requires careful planning. If you want your birthday child to join in this game, you must plan it without his help or knowledge.

A few days before the party, make a Treasure Chest (a box filled with favors for the guests). Decorate the chest by covering it with foil or spray-painting it gold or silver.

Good "treasures" for the chest are small bags of gold coin candy or little bags of colored jelly beans. Fancy fake jewel rings and other small toys from the variety store would be appropriate, too. (Whatever the treasures, each child should receive the same thing.) ⬚ Hide the Treasure Chest until the party, in a place where it won't get wet or damaged.

⬚ Now make up clues that will lead to the hidden treasure. One clue must lead to the next one, and this to the next, and so on until the final clue leads to the Treasure Chest. Make at least 6 clues, up to 10 if you can. Lots of clues make the Treasure Hunt more suspenseful and fun.

Print the clues on small pieces of paper. Fold the papers, and number them in the order in which they should be found. (If the treasure hunters are too young to read well, you can draw pictures for clues instead of writing directions. Or an adult can read the clues for them.)

⬚ **Important:** Before the party, test your Treasure Hunt trail. Follow the trail from clue to clue, checking to see that each one leads to the next in proper order.

At the party, give the first clue to a player, who reads it out loud. The clue might say, "Look in a cold place." The child decides to look in the refrigerator, or even in the ice cube section (all the treasure hunters go with her to search). There she will find the second clue, which another hunter gets to read. Each child should have a chance to read and figure out a clue.

The second clue may lead everybody outside by saying, "Swing high, swing low, that's where you will find me"—and they find the third clue tied to the backyard swing set. This clue may lead the children inside again ("Where do you bake a birthday cake?" In the oven, of course), or to the garage ("A car lives here"), or to a distant part of the yard.

Some possible hiding places for clues might be: under the kitchen sink ("Down the drain goes the dishwater"); tied to the garden hose ("I make it rain when you use me"); under a sofa pillow ("Sit on me—I'm soft"); under the front doormat ("Welcome to my house—step on me").

After the pirates have found their treasure, you can serve lunch. If there is time after the "Buried Treasure" birthday cake, the children can play "Pirate's Chest."

PIRATE'S CHEST. The children sit in a circle. One player begins the game by saying, "I opened the pirate's chest and I found . . . " He names something a pirate might use, such as a sword.

The next player must repeat what the first player said, and

add another thing from the pirate's chest, such as a boot or a gold coin.

As the game goes around the circle, each player must remember all the things that were named before, and add another thing to the list. If a player forgets one item, he leaves the game. The game goes on until only one player can name all the things in the pirate's chest.

The children may take home their eye patches, earrings, sashes, daggers, treasures, and a balloon.

SUMMER

This is a funny, quiet party that will prove a favorite. Everybody wins a prize in the animal contest, everybody gets a funny hat, everybody imitates an animal, everybody makes a mask, and everybody has a wonderful time.

Warm and sunny weather may invite you to move this party outdoors.

Theme

Animals, wild and tame, big and small. Colorful balloons add to the cheerful animal decorations.

Invitations

 See Basic Invitation, page xix. Use any color paper. In the center of the outside page, print the birthday child's name and the party theme: *Layne's Animal Fair*. Draw animal pictures on this page, or cut small pictures of animals from old magazines to paste around the printed words. Or use animal stamps from the stationery store.

Ask each guest to bring a favorite toy animal—there will be an animal contest.

Decorations

Make an animal collage for the front door. On a big sheet of paper or poster board, print the birthday child's name and the party theme, as on the invitations. Cut out pictures of animals (not too small) from old magazines, and paste these around the printed words (leave space between the words and the pictures). Tape or tack the collage to your front door.

Put toy animals all around the party room—stuffed, rubber, plastic, and wooden. The animals should sit on shelves, look down from curtain rods, peek from under chairs and out of cupboards and around doors, everywhere you can think of.

Blow up balloons and draw animal faces on them with permanent felt-tip markers (watercolor markers won't work on balloons). Tie a balloon to each child's chair at the table.

For the party table, make animal place mats out of brown paper or grocery bags. Cut the paper into rectangles, and draw a simple animal shape on each. Cut out the animal shapes if you like. Let the party guests color them later, at the table.

If you use paper plates and cups, draw animals on them with permanent felt-tip markers.

Favors

Place a box of crayons at each child's place. The children can color their place mats while waiting for lunch to be served.

Make animal party hats for the children. You will need:

cut-open grocery bags or strong construction paper (gray, brown, black, and white)

tape
a stapler
pencil
scissors (blunt safety)

1. For each hat, cut 3 strips of paper, each about 1 inch wide and 18 inches long. **2.** Wrap 1 strip around your child's head, and tape it together in the back to make a headband. If the strip is too short, stape or tape 2 strips together. To strengthen this headband, tape down a strip of masking tape or cellophane tape all along the inside. **3.** Put a strip of paper over the top of the head, side to side, and tape or staple this to the headband. Cut off any extra paper. **4.** Tape or staple another strip over the top, front to back, to make a cap of paper strips.

 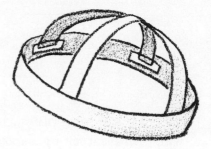

Cut ears out of the same color paper: make short pointy ears for cats, longer pointy ears for horses, long floppy ears for hound dogs, long stand-up ears for rabbits. Fold the ears to give them the right shape. (If the paper is not stiff enough to stand up straight, cut each ear from doubled paper and tape the pieces together.) Staple or tape the ears to the headband. Horse and dog ears go on the sides. Cat, mouse, and rabbit ears go toward the back of the head.

Print a child's name on each animal hat, and give each

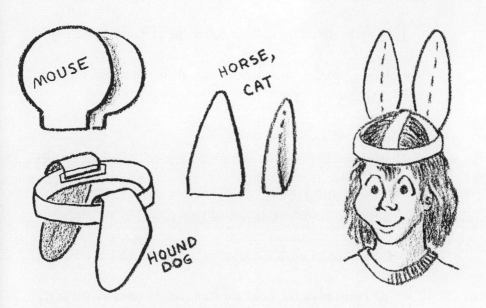

guest his hat as he arrives. If the headband does not fit, cut the tape in back and retape the band to fit.

Food

- Brown Cows (root beer poured over a scoop of vanilla ice cream in a tall glass)
- Rabbit Food (carrot and celery sticks)
- Little Corn Dogs (See recipe on page 97.)
- Zebra Cake (See recipe on page 98.)

Games

Two of the games have winners. Boxes of animal crackers would make good prizes.

ANIMAL CONTEST. The animals in this contest are the favorite toys the children brought to the party. Every toy animal will receive a blue ribbon.

Make the award ribbons before the party. You will need:

blue ribbon, 1 to 2 inches wide, about 12 inches for each
   animal
tape
letter paper or index cards
scissors (blunt safety, and sharp ones for adults to cut the
   ribbon)
pen or felt-tip marker
a rubber band for each award ribbon

Slip a ribbon through a rubber band and tie the ribbon into a
bow.

   On slips of paper, print the names of the awards. Make up
your own awards, or choose from this list: Biggest Animal,
Smallest Animal, Most Colorful Animal, Oldest Animal, Fuz-

ziest Animal, Smoothest Animal, Floppiest Animal, Longest Tail, Biggest Nose, Longest Ears, Strangest Animal, Best-Dressed Animal, Happiest Animal, Saddest Animal, Most Legs (someone may bring a spider), Fewest Legs (someone may bring a snake).

Staple or tape an award card to each blue bow. Make sure there are enough awards to go around!

Place all the toy animals in a line. Each animal's owner should stand behind it, as in a real dog show. The judge should be the adult party helper, so the birthday child can be in the contest, too. The judge walks down the line of toys, and decides which animal should receive which award. He then puts the rubber bands with the blue ribbons around the necks of the animals or tapes them to the toys.

GUESS WHAT ANIMAL I AM. The children should take off their animal hats while they play this game.

Cut slips of paper about 3 inches long and 1 inch wide. On each slip, print the name of a different animal: dog, donkey, worm, cat, elephant, kangaroo, bear, sheep, pig, mouse, cow, horse, lion, rabbit, frog, bee, snake, duck, rooster, alligator, monkey, fish, butterfly, grasshopper, dinosaur. Fold the slips of paper and put them into a paper bag.

The children sit on one side of the room. The first player reaches into the bag and takes out a slip of paper. He silently reads the name of the animal (or the adult helper whispers the name to him). The player tries to act like that animal. He may make the animal's sounds, but he may not say its name.

The other children try to guess what animal the actor is supposed to be. When someone guesses the right animal, the next child takes her turn. If there are enough animal names, the children could play this game again.

SCORPION. For this game, you will need a record or tape player or a bell to ring, and a small toy scorpion or spider (or any small item, such as a peanut). The leader (adult party helper) plays the music.

The players sit in a circle, facing the center. The leader begins to play music (or rings the bell), and the children pass the scorpion around from hand to hand.

Suddenly the music stops. The player who is caught holding the scorpion is "stung," and must leave the game. The music starts again, and the rest of the players pass the scorpion around as fast as they can—no one wants to be stung when the music stops! The game goes on until there is only one player left, the winner.

PUT THE TAIL ON THE BUNNY. This is a version of Pin the Tail on the Donkey.

Draw the bunny on a sheet of poster board or cardboard. Use cotton balls as tails, one for each player. Put a small loop of tape, sticky side out (or use double-faced tape), on each cotton ball. To identify the bunny tails, you may tape small numbered tags to them when you apply the sticky tape.

Tape or tack the bunny picture against the wall at one end of the party room. The children stand at the other end. Blindfold the first player and give her a bunny tail. Turn her around three times, and point her toward the bunny.

Holding the tail out in front of herself, with the tape pointed toward the bunny, the player tries to tape her bunny tail as close as she can to the tail position on the picture. She must use only one hand, and must leave the tail wherever it first touches.

The player who places a bunny tail closest to the right spot wins the prize.

ANIMAL MASKS. Follow the directions for Scary Masks (pages 79–80), but draw animal faces instead.

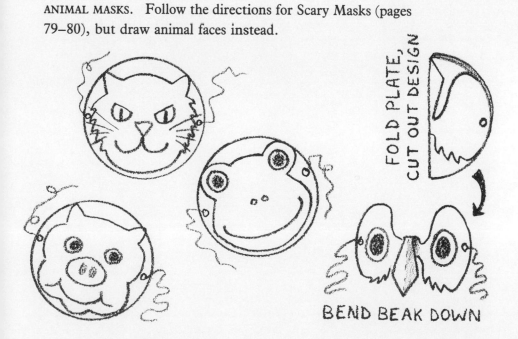

While the guests wait for lunch to be served, they can color their animal place mats with the crayon favors they find at their places.

If there is time after the birthday cake, read an animal story to the children. Or they can sing songs while wearing their animal hats. Some appropriate songs would be: "Old Mac-Donald Had a Farm," "Baa, Baa, Black Sheep," "The Bear Went Over the Mountain," and "I Had a Bird." (You probably can think of several more.)

The children may take home their party hats, blue ribbon awards, animal masks, place mats and crayons, and a balloon.

Peanuts, more peanuts, and still *more* peanuts! This party is full of them, in the decorations, prizes, food and games. At the end of the party, the children can learn a special, old-time "Peanut Song." Most of the activities can be moved indoors in bad weather.

Theme

Peanuts, circus clowns, and elephants. Bright yellow, red, and blue are circus colors.

Invitations

 See Basic Invitation, page xix. Use yellow paper. Draw a big peanut shape on the outside. You could cut out around

the peanut shape, being careful not to cut through the folded side. Print the birthday child's name and the party theme on the peanut: *Tom's Peanut Circus Party.*

Advise the invited guests to wear old clothes for outside play.

Decorations

Tie bright balloons to trees and backyard furniture. If the party is to be indoors, tape circus posters around the room. Or make big drawings of elephants on large sheets of craft paper or cut-open grocery bags, and tape these around the party area.

To make a sign for your front door, draw a picture of an elephant's head on a big sheet of paper or poster board. Tape a peanut to the end of the trunk. Below this, print the birthday child's name and the party theme, as on the invitations. Tape the sign to your front door.

Favors

For each young guest, make some soap-bubble mixture (half a cup of water with a few teaspoons of dish detergent mixed in) and a wire wand for forming the bubbles. Containers for the mixture may be small margarine tubs with lids, or small jars with screw tops. Plastic margarine tubs may leak; use these only for outdoor play.

To make the wands, cut pieces of wire about 20 inches long. Twist the wire to make a loop, and twist the ends into a handle. Wrap tape around the cut ends for safety.

Give these favors to the children after the birthday cake.

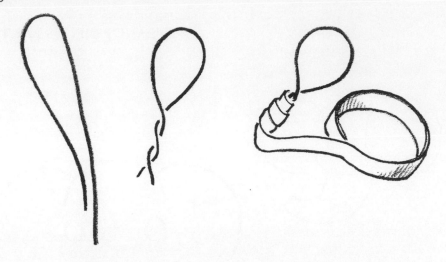

The children can blow bubbles around the yard before they leave, then take the bubble mixture home with them.

Make party hats from bright-colored paper. Or use craft paper or cut-open grocery bags, and add colors later.

To make a pointed hat, cut a sheet of paper 15 inches wide and 18 inches long. Fold it into the shape shown below. You could draw or paint designs on the hats, or paste on cotton

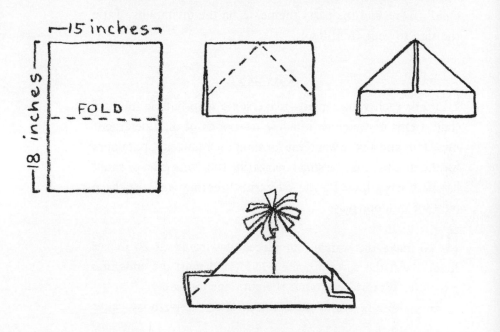

balls or paper streamers or stars. To make a pompom for the top, cut 4 to 6 narrow strips of paper, and tie the strips tightly in the middle. Tape the pompom to the point of the hat, and then gently fluff out the strips.

A different style of hat can be made with crepe paper. To make a crepe paper hat: 1. Wrap a length of paper around your child's head once, to determine the right measure. 2. Cut off the paper where it overlaps. 3. Sew or staple along the cut edges to make a tall tube. 4. Fold the outside of the paper tube down, and put the tube back on the child with the fold at the ears, the cut edges at the top. 5. Pinch the doubled tube at the crown of the head and tie it with a ribbon or string. You may snip the top part into a fringe, if you like.

The children must stay out of the backyard until all have arrived. While painting Clown Faces on the childen is not, strictly speaking, a party favor, it adds to the party theme and keeps the guests together. ⌷ You can buy real theatrical "grease sticks," or you can make your own face paint. You will need:

½ cup flour
6 tablespoons cornstarch
2 cups cool water
food colors

1. Sift the flour and cornstarch into a saucepan. 2. Add the water gradually, stirring the mixture smooth. 3. Stir this over medium heat until it comes to a boil. 4. Remove from heat and let the mixture cool. 5. Divide it among several small bowls, and stir a few drops of different food color into each bowl. This makeup will wash off with soap and water; recipe makes about 2 cups.

Food

- Orange Pop (orange juice and soda water)
- Popcorn
- Peanut butter sandwiches, with various fillings to be added by the children as they wish. Pile a tray with plain peanut butter sandwiches, cut in half. On a sheet or blanket spread on the grass, put the tray of sandwiches and bowls of different fillings, such as slices of banana, jelly, bacon bits, raisins. (You may have to help young children with the fillings.)
- Frosted birthday cupcakes (Decorate with colored sugar or sprinkles and put a candle on each cupcake. Group the cakes on a tray so the birthday child can blow out the candles, or allow the children to blow out their candles all at the same time.)

• Clown ice cream cones  (Make these the day before the party, and freeze on a sheet of waxed paper on a tray. Serve the cones right from the tray.)

To make clown cones: Use any flavor ice cream. **1.** On a tray, set out a paper baking cup for each child. These will be the collars for the clown heads. **2.** With an ice cream scoop, put a round ball of ice cream into each cup. **3.** Place an ice cream cone on top of each ball at a slight angle. **4.** Freeze the ice cream balls hard.

To make the clown faces, work on only 2 or 3 ice cream balls at a time, keeping the rest in the freezer. Use chocolate chips or raisins for eyes and noses, and slices of raisin or candied cherry for smiling mouths. Place a row of chocolate chips or chocolate sprinkles around the edge of the cone for hair. Top the cone with a cherry. Return the clown cones to the freezer until ready to serve.

Games

Some of the games are contests. Be sure the prizes have something to do with peanuts—such as packets of peanut butter crackers or peanut butter candy bars.

GREAT PEANUT HUNT. Several hours before the party, hide about 200 peanuts-in-the-shell all over the backyard. Leave some in plain sight, hide others in various places. Do not hide the peanuts too early, however, or squirrels and birds may make off with them.

Give each child a small paper bag and allow 15 or 20 minutes to collect the peanuts. The winner is the child who finds the most peanuts.

DROP THE PEANUT. This is a circle game. One player is chosen to be "It" and holds a peanut. The rest of the children form a circle, facing in. They hold their hands behind them with palms up, and begin to chant, "Drop the peanut! Drop the peanut!"

The player who is "It" walks fast around the outside of the circle. Suddenly, she drops the peanut into someone's hand and begins to run around the circle. The player with the peanut must run after her and try to tag her before she reaches the open space in the circle.

If "It" reaches the open space without being tagged, she stays in the circle and the other player becomes the new "It." If "It" gets tagged before she reaches the open space, however, she must remain "It" for another turn. The game goes on until the players get tired.

TIGHTROPE WALKING. Stretch a length of rope along the ground and fasten it in place with weights or pegs. The players stand at one end of the rope. The first player holds a big spoon in each hand. Place a peanut in each spoon. Holding his arms out wide, the player must walk the length of the rope without dropping the peanuts. (There may be more than one winner to this game.)

PEANUT RELAY RACE. There should be an even number of players in this game. The children form two teams at one end of the yard. Put a goal at the other end, such as a box or chair to run around.

The teams line up. Give a peanut to the first player in each line. These players must hold the peanut between upper lip and nose—without using their hands—and hop to the goal at the far end of the yard. Here they must get down on hands and knees and crawl back to their teams.

Now the next players in line take the peanuts, put them in position, and hop away. The winning team is the one whose members finish first.

After lunch and birthday cupcakes, the children can learn to sing "The Peanut Song." They can blow soap bubbles around the yard until it is time to leave. They may take home their party hat, soap bubble mixture and wand, and a balloon.

The Peanut Song
(to the tune of "My Darling Clementine")

Found a peanut, found a peanut, found a peanut just now,
   I just now found a peanut, found a peanut just now.
Broke it open, broke it open, broke it open just now,
   I just now broke it open, broke it open just now.
It was rotten . . . (etc.)
Ate it anyway . . .
Got sick . . .
Called the doctor . . .
Died anyhow . . .

Went to heaven . . .
Played a harp . . .
Struck a sour note . . .
Went to hell . . .
Shoveled coal . . .
Got burned . . .
Burned to fertilizer . . .
Grew a peanut, grew a peanut, grew a peanut just now.
    I just now grew a peanut, grew a peanut just now.

Autumn

Boo! This is a wonderful, creepy party you might like to stage even if no one has an autumn birthday. The centerpiece is the Haunted House. This takes time, and some help, to put together, but it's so much fun that once you do it, you may want to repeat the party year after year.

Unless you have a basement room you can darken during the day, you should plan this party for late afternoon or evening, with supper afterwards. You could take the children outside to play a lively game before it gets too dark. Since this is a haunted *house*, though, and an evening party, it works best as an indoor event.

Theme

Scary things such as ghosts, witches, and bats; bare trees, dead leaves, autumn colors. Balloons should be white, and perhaps orange and yellow.

Invitations

See Basic Invitation, page xix. Use gray or orange construction paper. With black crayon or marker, draw an owl with its head and wings touching the fold of the paper. Print the birthday child's name and the party theme below the owl: *Matt's Haunted House Party*. You could cut away part of the design along the heavy lines, as shown.

Ask the invited guests to *please arrive exactly on time*. If you plan to serve supper, say so on the invitation.

Decorations

The Haunted House takes time and help to set up (suggestions for setting it up begin on page 73). Line up adults or older brothers and sisters to help during the party. They will guide the party guests through the darkened room and do some of the tricks.

On a large sheet of paper, print the party sign in creepy black letters:

HAUNTED HOUSE
KNOCK 3 TIMES

Crumple the paper, flatten it out again, and tape it to your front door.

Decorate the party table with autumn colors—red, orange, yellow, brown. Or use only orange and black. You can put bright autumn leaves on the table. Tie white, yellow, or orange balloons to the chairs. Draw ghosts, bats, and "Boo!" on the inflated balloons with permanent felt-tip markers (watercolor markers won't work on balloons).

Put a sheet of black construction paper at each place, for place mats. Add a piece of chalk to each setting, too, so the guests can draw on the black paper while they wait for the food to be served.

Favors

Make a little bag of "magic charms" for each guest. You will need:

> black cloth (each bag requires 11 square inches; you can make 12 bags from one yard of 45-inch-wide cloth)
> orange yarn
> a large-eye darning needle
> dinner plate, 10 or 11 inches in diameter
> white pencil or chalk
> scissors (sharp, for cutting fabric)
> "charms" to put in the bags: "witch's teeth" (candy corn), small boxes of raisins or pretzels, chewy candy "worms"

1. Spread out the black cloth. **2.** Place the dinner plate upside down on the cloth and draw around it. Draw as many circles as you have party guests. **3.** Cut out the cloth circles; the cut edges do not have to be smooth. **4.** Thread the darning needle with a piece of yarn 12 inches long. **5.** Sew around the edge of a cloth circle, about 1 inch in from the edge, ending on the same side of the cloth where you started. **6.** Draw up the yarn to make a little bag. Repeat with all the cloth circles.

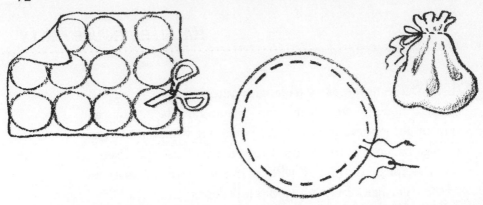

Fill the bags with charms and tie them closed. Place a bag at each table setting.

Food

- Purple Poison (grape juice and ginger ale, mixed)
- Applesauce
- Carrot sticks
- Pickles
- Magic Circle Hot Dogs (See recipe on page 99.)
- Ketchup and mustard
- Ice cream
- Spiderweb Cake (A layer cake or sheet cake with chocolate or orange frosting, with a spider's web drawn in white icing. Construct a spider from a marshmallow and 8 pipe cleaners, its eyes made from chocolate frosting or little candies held on with dabs of frosting.)

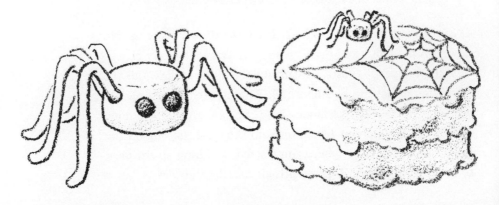

Haunted House

The Haunted House should be as scary as possible. It should have a ghost or two, bats to fly in the air, cobwebs, and a stuffed "body." Make all these things a day or two before the party.

GHOST. You will need a large balloon, an old white sheet, and some string for hanging the ghost. **1.** Blow up the balloon and tie it closed. **2.** Hold the balloon knot-side up and drape the sheet over it. **3.** Tie a string around the knot and the bit of sheet that covers the knot. **4.** Cut two eyes from black paper and tape these in place on the ghost's face.

Hang the ghost from a light fixture, or from a long string stretched across the room, above eye level. You can sew a long thread to the bottom of the ghost; a helper can pull this ever so slightly to make the ghost move.

STUFFED BODY. Stuff some old clothes with crumpled newspaper. Safety-pin the parts together. Use a crumpled, stuffed paper bag for the head, and put a hat on top. Place the body in a corner where it won't be seen clearly.

BATS. Cut bats out of black paper. Paint on eyes, if you like, with white poster paint. Hang the bats on threads around the room, in doorways and from curtain rods. If your Haunted House is in the attic or basement, you may be able to hang bats and the ghosts from the rafters, or tack the threads into the ceiling.

COBWEBS. 1. Cut a piece of string a little longer than the width of the doorway to the Haunted House room. 2. Stretch the string along the floor or a table top. 3. Cut many lengths, 30 or more, of strong black thread, about 9 feet long. 4. Tie each thread at its middle to the string (space the threads along the string).

You will have a long string of dangling black threads. Tack this at the top of the doorway. In the dark, the threads will feel like cobwebs when they touch the children's faces. (Of course, you will tell everyone the cobwebs are real, and wonder out loud where the spiders are hiding.)

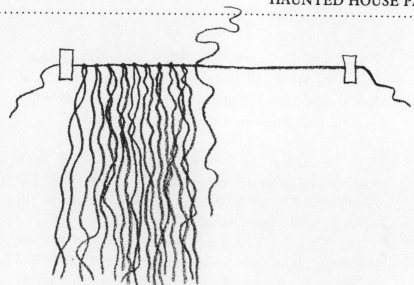

The only lights should be a few flashlights. Place these in corners and behind chairs, so the room is very dim and things are hard to see. This will make the ghost and bats look spooky, and it will be harder to tell what is real and what is only make-believe.

Practice the tricks of your Haunted House before the party. Make sure you know when to do each thing, and that all the tricks will work.

Caution: No child should have to play Haunted House if he doesn't want to. Make-believe scaring can be a lot of fun, but not for everyone. A child who doesn't want to play can wait for this part of the party to end before joining in the rest of the fun. He could draw or cut out paper owls and bats while he waits in another, lighted room.

Greet the children as they arrive at the front door. All the lights should be off; lead the guests in with a flashlight. Take them to a room where they will leave their coats and wait for all to arrive before the Haunted House game begins. You could tell a ghost story while waiting.

The children should have to crawl through a dark tunnel to reach the Haunted House room. Make this tunnel out of blankets draped over chairs. You can put a string of "cobwebs" across the end of the tunnel to make it more scary.

As the children crawl out of the tunnel, a Witch (adult helper dressed in black) shakes hands with each child. The Witch's "hand" is really an empty glove with twigs in the fingers, so it feels like a withered, bony hand.

The Witch slowly leads the children to the middle of the room while she or someone else secretly moves the ghost and fans the paper bats to make them flutter. Meanwhile, another helper, out of sight, makes scary noises: shrieks (stretch the neck of an inflated balloon and let the air out slowly); dry bones (tie some wooden spoons together loosely and shake them); eerie music (open the piano and stroke an empty bottle across the strings, or do the same with a guitar); rattling chains (shake a big bunch of keys).

The Witch speaks in a high, creepy voice, telling the children all about the noises and pointing out the ghost, stuffed body, and bats, which can just barely be seen in the dim light.

Then the children all sit in a circle, and the games begin.

Games

The first game, Frankenstein's Body, may be too scary for some 5- and 6-year-old children. For these younger children, you can skip this game and tell a ghost story and sing songs instead. Then turn on the lights and play the rest of the non-scary games.

FRANKENSTEIN'S BODY. ☐ The Witch invites the children to become members of the Haunted House Society. In order to do this, they must pass a test.

But first they must all put on blindfolds, the Witch says, "because what comes next is too horrible to see." She ties blindfolds on all the children.

"Frankenstein died last year, and I dug him up last night," says the Witch. "Here are parts of his body, which I am going to pass around."

She carries one item at a time around the circle of children for them to feel.

These are the parts of Frankenstein:

his entrails (bowl of cold, cooked, slimy macaroni)
teeth (large kernels of hard corn)
eyes (large peeled grapes)
lungs (cold wet sponges)
heart (balloon filled with cold water, about the size of a large
   fist; this wet balloon should be placed in the hand of a
   victim so he doesn't feel the knot)

After all the children have felt the parts of Frankenstein, and have stopped giggling and squealing, the Witch tells them they have passed the first test.

Next she must "brand" them on the forehead with a hot

iron, and they will be official members of the Haunted House Society. She touches each child with an ice cube. Now they may take off their blindfolds.

The Witch gives each new Haunted House Society member a badge. Make the badges by cutting a bat shape from black or gray paper. Print "HHS" on one side. On the back, put a loop of tape, sticky side out (or use double-faced tape), and press the badge to the child's shirt.

NONSCARY GAMES. If you think you may have another Haunted House party next year, and want to keep your tricks and props secret, take the children to another room to play the rest of the games. If this will be a once-in-a-lifetime party, you can just turn on the lights and proceed.

GREAT GHOST HUNT. The children hunt for paper ghosts hidden around the room. You will need:

> white paper
> pencil
> scissors (blunt safety)

Draw 25 simple little ghosts about 2 inches high on a sheet of paper. Holding 4 sheets of paper together, cut out the ghosts you have drawn on the top sheet. You will have 100 ghosts. Draw eyes on each, if you like.

Before the party, hide the paper ghosts all around the room. You can slide some under the edge of the rug, tape some to the back of curtains, put some under cushions.

At the party, tell the children, "This house really is haunted. In fact, there are little ghosts all over the room." Give the children 15 or 20 minutes to hunt. The child who finds the most ghosts wins a small prize, such as a rubber snake or toy spider.

SCARY MASKS. You will need:

    plain paper plates, 2 or 3 for each child
    string
    several pairs of safety scissors
    crayons or felt-tip markers
    a stapler
    colored paper, bits of yarn and ribbon

1. The children draw scary or funny faces on the paper plates.
2. Hold the mask up to a child's face, and have him touch two
fingers to his eyes through the paper. Mark these positions
with a crayon. Then cut eye holes in the faces, and cut off the
edges to shape the masks, if necessary. 3. Color the masks;
tape or staple on bits of yarn, ribbon, paper strips to make
hair, mustaches, and beards. 4. Staple string ties to the sides,
and tie the masks on the children.

FOLD PLATE, CUT OUT DESIGN

BEND NOSE DOWN

After the games, serve the spooky supper. The children
may take home their masks, bags of Magic Charms, the
Haunted House Society badges, and a balloon.

This lively party includes a funny play. There is a part for every child—and no need for practicing! The cowboy bandanna favors will be the props for the play. Everything is Wild West: food, decorations, and games. Most of the games can be played indoors if the weather turns bad.

Themes

Old Western, with cowboys, horses, cattle, ropes, and wagon wheels. Use brown and red in your decorations, for a "leather," outdoorsy feel.

Invitations

See Basic Invitation, page xix. Use light brown paper or cut-up grocery bags. With black crayon or marker, print the birthday child's name and the party theme in the center of the outside page: *Nell's Western Bar-B-Q Party*. Draw cattle brands all around the words.

On the invitations, ask the children to wear outdoor clothes (blue jeans and flannel shirts, if possible).

Decorations

Make a Western sign for your front door. On a large sheet of brown craft paper or a cut-open grocery bag, print the birthday child's name and the party theme, as on the invitations. You can draw a longhorn steer around the words, or draw more cattle brands. Cut the bottom of the paper to make a "leather" fringe.

Turkey Track   Horse Track   Triangle   Broken Arrow   Spur

Sunset   Bow and Arrow   Running W   Stirrup   Flying Heart

For the party table, make place mats out of more grocery bags. Fringe the ends of the place mats, and draw a cattle brand on each.

Have plenty of red balloons at the party; some will be used in a game.

Favors

Give each child a cowboy bandanna to wear. These will be used in the first game, as props.

Buy bandannas or make them. For 2 bandannas, you will need ⅔ yard of bright-printed cotton fabric, 45 inches wide. Simply cut the fabric in half; hemming is not necessary.

One of the good things to eat at a Bar-B-Q is Trail Mix.

Make a "leather" pouch for each child so he can carry his Trail Mix around with him.

You will need:

small rectangles of brown felt, about 8½ by 11 inches (available at variety or fabric stores; one rectangle makes 2 pouches)

scissors (sharp, for cutting the felt)

needle and thread, or fabric glue

twine or yarn

Trail Mix (a mixture of shelled peanuts, raisins, popcorn, and coated candies)

1. Cut a felt rectangle in half the long way. 2. Fold one piece in half. 3. Sew or glue the sides together to make a little bag

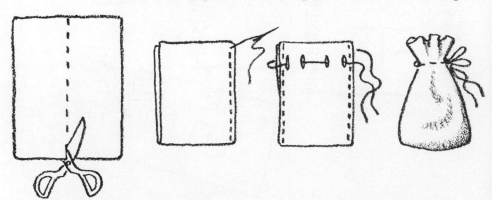

(let the glue dry before filling the bag). **4.** About one inch down from the top, cut 8 tiny slits all around the bag. **5.** Cut a piece of twine or yarn 12 inches long. **6.** Thread the twine through the slits to make a drawstring.

Fill the pouches with Trail Mix and tie them closed. Place a pouch at each table setting.

__Food__

- Cow Punch (milk)
- Fresh Fruit Cup (pieces of apple, banana, orange, and grapes, in a cup)
- Potato chips
- Bar-B-Q on a Bun (See recipe on page 100; make the meat filling the day before the party.)
- Ice cream

- Wagon Wheel Birthday Cake (a round, frosted cake decorated to look like a wheel, with rim, spokes, and center hub drawn in a contrasting color of icing)

Games

Two games will have prizewinners. Count the number of possible winners before you buy prizes. Small toy horses or books about the West would be appropriate.

As the children arrive, give each one a bandanna to tie around his neck, cowboy-style. These will be used in the play, and also in one of the active games.

STAGECOACH ROBBERY. After all the children have arrived, stage a play. Everyone will be an actor but no one has to practice for this play. These are the characters and what they say:

Driver ("Giddyap! giddyap!")
Horses ("Gallop, gallop, gallop!")
Passengers ("Heavens to Betsy! Heavens to Betsy!")
Robbers ("Reach for the sky!")
Cowboy Dan ("Howdy, pardner!")
Storyteller (This is an adult who will read the story aloud)

There may be several horses, passengers, and robbers, or only one of each, depending on the number of children at the party.

The different characters use their bandannas to show who they are in the play: the Robbers tie their bandannas across their mouths and noses for masks; the Passengers tie their bandannas over their heads for hats; the Horses tie their bandannas on top of their heads for ears; the Driver ties his bandanna behind his neck; and Cowboy Dan ties his bandanna in front.

The actors all sit in a circle while the Storyteller reads the story of a stagecoach trip. Every time a character is mentioned, that character must jump up and shout her line out loudly.

For instance, all the horses jump up and shout, "Gallop, gallop, gallop!" when they hear the word *horse;* the Robbers jump up and shout, "Reach for the sky!" when they hear the word *robber;* and so on. The players should try saying their parts once before the play begins, to be sure they know what to do. The Storyteller may add to the play if he likes, to make it longer. The more often the different characters are mentioned, the more fun the play becomes.

The Story of a Stagecoach Robbery

The stagecoach is ready to leave Dodge City on its way to Dry Gulch. The *horses* are hitched up, and the stagecoach *driver* comes. The *driver* opens the door for the *passengers.* The *horses* stamp their feet and whinny. Now the *passengers* climb into the stagecoach. The *driver* shouts to the *horses* and cracks his whip, and off they go.

The *horses* trot along, up the hills and down the valleys. The *passengers* hold onto their seats as the *driver* cracks his whip and calls to the *horses*, and the stagecoach bounces along. When the *horses* pull the stagecoach across a shallow river, the water splashes the *passengers*, and they call up to the *driver*. The *driver* shouts to his *horses*, and the *horses* run faster. The *horses* gallop around a sharp curve, and the *passengers* bump against each other. The *passengers* call out to the *driver* to slow down. The *driver* at last slows down his *horses*. The *passengers* call out "Thank you!" to the *driver*, and the *horses* trot on down the road.

Suddenly, the *driver* hears the sound of galloping *horses* behind him! The *driver* looks back and sees a gang of *robbers* racing toward the stagecoach! The *driver* shouts to his *horses* and cracks the whip, and the *horses* tear down the road. Now the *passengers* can see the *robbers*, too, and they call to the *driver* to make the *horses* run faster! All the *horses* thunder along with the stagecoach rocking from side to side, while the frightened *passengers* bounce around inside. The *robbers* are gaining on the stagecoach! The *driver* cracks his whip again and again, but the poor *horses* are too tired to run any faster.

The *robbers* ride up beside the stagecoach. They call to the *driver* to stop his *horses*. The *horses* slow down to a walk, and then stop. The *driver* climbs down from his seat. The *robbers* make the *passengers* get out and stand in the middle of the road. The *robbers* get off their *horses*.

Now there is a new sound—the thunder of a *horse's* hooves! The *passengers* and the *driver* and the *robbers* all look down the road, and see our hero, *Cowboy Dan*!

Cowboy Dan races up to the stagecoach, whirling his lasso around his head. The *robbers* try to get back on their *horses*, but they are too late. *Cowboy Dan* ropes all the *robbers* with one throw. The *driver* runs to help *Cowboy Dan* tie up the *robbers,* while the *passengers* cheer and the *horses* stamp their feet.

Cowboy Dan ties the *robbers' horses* to the back of the stagecoach. The *passengers* get back into the stagecoach and the *driver* climbs back to his seat. The *driver* takes up the reins again, and calls to the *horses.* The stagecoach moves off down the road with the *robbers' horses* following along behind.

Cowboy Dan rides behind the stagecoach, pulling the tied-up *robbers* along the dusty road. The *passengers* in the stagecoach laugh and cheer "Hooray for *Cowboy Dan!*" all the way to the Dry Gulch jail.

LASSO THE STEER.   First, make a steer. **1.** Tie 2 long sticks (or 2 brooms) together to make an "X." This will be the horns of the steer. **2.** Place the crossed sticks against a chair so the "horns" lean across the seat and poke up over the back of the chair; see the illustration below. **3.** Tie the crossed sticks firmly

in place so they won't slip out of position. **4.** Cover the back of the chair and the "horns" with a large paper bag; cut holes in the bag for the "horns" to poke through. You may draw a steer face on the bag. **6.** Drape a blanket over the chair, for the steer's hide.

Next, make the lassos. Cut pieces of rope about 18 inches long, and tie them in circles. (To make bigger lassos, cut longer pieces of rope.) You will need three lassos.

To play the game, the players stand about six feet away from the steer and take turns tossing the lassos at its horns. Each child gets three tries, using all three lassos. (If this is too easy, have the children stand farther away.)

If more than one child rings the horns with all three lassos, they move back and try again, until only one child can lasso the steer three times in a row: the winner.

THREE-LEGGED PONY RACE. The players race in pairs, with two legs tied together at the knees and ankles (or only at the knees, for younger players). Use their bandannas to tie the players' legs together. The "ponies" may want to practice walking for a minute before they try to race. They will be able to keep their balance better if they put their arms around each other's shoulders.

The pairs of children line up at one end of the backyard. (Some neighs and a few whinnies may be expected here.) At

a signal, they all race to a line at the other end of the yard. If the backyard is small, have the ponies race around a base and back to the starting line. The first pair of players to reach the finish line wins the race.

HERDING CATTLE. This is a relay race, with teams of players. There should be an even number of players for this game.

Set up an obstacle course, using chairs to go under, trees and bushes to go around, grocery cartons opened at both ends to go through. With a ball of twine or a sifter full of flour, make a trail along this course, all around the backyard, and back to the starting point.

The players form two teams at the starting point. Give the first player on each team a balloon and a whisk broom. The players must herd their balloon "cows" along the trail, touching their "cows" only with the whisk brooms. The balloons may wander off in all directions, just as real cattle do. If a player's balloon should burst, that player must run back to the starting line for another, and begin again at the start of the trail. (On a very windy day, you could use soccer-size balls in place of the balloons.) The first team to finish herding its cattle wins the game.

After the games, the children may cool down before lunch by singing a cowboy song, such as "Home on the Range." If there is time after the birthday cake, an adult could read a cowboy story to the group. The children may take home their bandannas, a balloon, and their pouches of Trail Mix (refilled for the long trail home).

Birthday Party Recipes

A birthday may be a time when you want to trot out a special treat that's your child's favorite. But you shouldn't feel obliged to go all-out with complicated or new dishes. Children at a party are too excited to be all that interested in new tastes, and will love familiar dishes. With all the party preparations you undertake, this may also be a time to save yourself and use some of the ready-to-serve sauces, cake mixes, and even bakery cakes that cut down time in the kitchen. After all, the true star of the party table will be . . . the cake with the candles for blowing good wishes.

Little Pizzas
(Snowflake Party)

1 can (7½ ounces) refrigerator biscuits (10 biscuits)
1 can (8 ounces) tomato sauce
1 teaspoon dried oregano leaves, crumbled
20 slices pepperoni
1 cup (4 ounces) shredded mozzarella cheese

1. Heat oven to 450° F.
2. Lightly grease 2 cookie sheets.
3. Separate biscuit dough into 10 biscuits.
Arrange 5 biscuits on each cookie sheet, leaving plenty of space between them. With lightly floured fingertips, pat each biscuit into a 4-inch round and pinch a ¼-inch-high rim around each edge.
4. Spread a scant tablespoon tomato sauce in the bottom of each biscuit. Sprinkle sauce with oregano; top with 2 cut-up slices pepperoni and some cheese.
5. Bake 5 to 7 minutes until edges are golden brown. Serve immediately.

Makes 10 little pizzas.

Orange-Applesauce Gelatin
(Snowflake Party)

3 cups water
2 packages (3 ounces each) orange gelatin
2 cups applesauce

1. Bring water to a boil in a saucepan.
2. Meanwhile, put gelatin into a medium-size bowl.
3. Pour boiling water over gelatin and stir about 3 minutes until completely dissolved.
4. Chill until slightly thickened.
5. Fold in applesauce. Pour into 13 x 9–inch dish or pan.
6. Refrigerate at least 3 hours or until firm.
7. Unmold and cut into cubes.

Makes 8 servings.

Spaghetti with Meatballs

(Art Party)

Meatballs

½ cup packaged seasoned dry bread crumbs
¼ cup water
12 ounces lean ground beef
1 large egg
1 tablespoon olive or vegetable oil

Sauce and Spaghetti

1 cup frozen chopped onions
1 jar (about 32 ounces) plain spaghetti sauce
1 cup cherry tomatoes (6 ounces), halved
1 pound spaghetti

1. To make meatballs, stir bread crumbs and water in a medium-size bowl. Let stand 3 minutes to soften.
2. Add ground beef and egg and mix until well blended. Form

level tablespoonfuls into 1-inch balls (you will have about 24 meatballs).

3. Heat oil in a 4-quart Dutch oven over medium-high heat. Add meatballs in a single layer. Cook 8 to 10 minutes, shaking or stirring 3 or 4 times, until meatballs are browned and barely pink in centers. With slotted spoon remove to a plate.

4. Stir onions into drippings in Dutch oven. Cook 3 to 5 minutes until crisp-tender.

5. Gently stir in spaghetti sauce, meatballs, and cherry tomatoes and bring to a boil. Reduce heat to medium-low, cover and simmer 8 to 10 minutes, stirring twice, until meatballs are firm and no longer pink in centers.

6. Meanwhile, bring a large pot of water to a boil over high heat. Add spaghetti and cook according to package directions, stirring frequently, until tender but still firm to the bite. Drain in a colander.

7. Transfer spaghetti to a large heated serving platter. Spoon meatballs and sauce over pasta. Serve immediately.

Serves 6 to 8 children.

Pirate Patties

(Pirate Party)

2 cans (about 15½ ounces each) corned or roast beef hash
2 teaspoons butter or oil for frying
Tomato ketchup

1. Chill the cans of hash several hours or overnight. Open both ends of each can, discarding one lid. Run a knife blade around the inside of the can to loosen the hash. Then push the reserved lid against the contents, forcing out the chilled hash in one piece. With a sharp knife, cut the contents of each can into 4 or 5 slices.

2. Heat butter or oil in skillet.

3. Fry the slices gently, turning once to brown both sides.

4. Serve with ketchup.

Makes 8 to 10 patties.

Little Corn Dogs

(Animal Fair Party)

1 package (11½ ounces) refrigerator cornbread sticks
32 cocktail-size hot dogs
Mustard

1. Heat oven to 375° F.

2. Unroll the refrigerator dough and separate it into 16 pieces.

3. Cut each piece in half.

4. Wrap one hot dog in each piece of dough.

5. Place on cookie sheet, carefully tucking the ends of the dough under each hot dog.

6. Bake 14 to 16 minutes or until golden brown.

7. Serve hot, with mustard.

Makes 32 little corn dogs.

No-Bake Zebra Cake
(Animal Fair Party)

You can make this ahead. Cover it with plastic wrap and freeze until firm. Allow 1 hour for thawing it in the refrigerator before serving.

1 teaspoon vanilla extract
1 container (8 ounces) frozen whipped topping, thawed or 2
    cups heavy cream, whipped with 2 teaspoons granulated
    sugar
1 package (8½ ounces) chocolate wafers

1. Stir vanilla extract into topping or whipped cream.

2. Spread the wafers with topping, saving enough to frost the cake, putting them together in stacks of 4 or 5. When all the wafers are spread and stacked, turn the stacks on their sides and press together into one long log.

3. Frost the log with reserved topping.

4. Chill 4 to 6 hours.

5. To serve: Slice diagonally at a 45-degree angle to make zebra-striped slices.

Serves 12.

Magic Circle Hot Dogs
(Haunted House Party)

Hot dogs
Hamburger buns
Oil for frying
Toothpicks
Tomato ketchup or mustard
Pickles

1. Slash a hot dog along one side in 5 places, almost but not quite through to the other side. Carefully bend the hot dog into a circle and secure with toothpicks.

2. Gently fry the hot dog on both sides in a bit of oil.

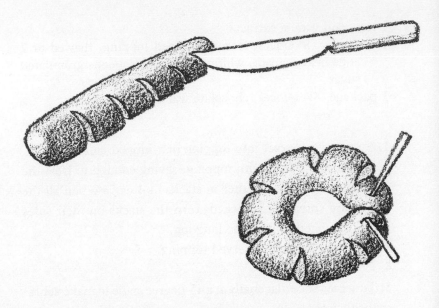

3. Place on a bun; remove toothpicks.

4. Serve with ketchup or mustard and a round slice of pickle in the center hole.

Bar-B-Q on a Bun
(Western Bar-B-Q Party)

This zippy barbecued beef is good reheated.

2 tablespoons butter or margarine
2 pounds ground beef
1 medium-size onion, minced
1 cup water
2 tablespoons cider vinegar
2 tablespoons brown sugar
¼ cup lemon juice
1 bottle (14 ounces) tomato ketchup

2 tablespoons Worcestershire sauce
½ teaspoon dry mustard
1 cup chopped celery
Salt and pepper to taste
6 toasted split hamburger buns

1. Melt butter in a large skillet.
2. Add beef and onion and cook over medium heat, breaking
up meat with a fork, until it loses its red color.
3. Add remaining ingredients, except buns.
4. Simmer, uncovered, stirring occasionally, 10 minutes, or
until celery is tender.
5. Serve on buns.

Makes 6 servings.

Cake Frostings

Ready-to-use canned frosting keeps well, and is handy to use—
and it's a great time-saver. Here are some tips on frosting, plus
instructions for basic icing, if you wish to make your own.

Cakes: Brush any loose crumbs from the surface of the cake
before you spread it with frosting. If you freeze the cake first,
it will be easier to handle.

Cupcakes: Dip the tops in the bowl of frosting. As you lift out
cupcakes, give each a twist to make the frosting swirl.

Buttercream Frosting

½ cup *each* solid vegetable shortening and butter or margarine
1 teaspoon vanilla extract
1 box (16 ounces) confectioners' sugar (about 4 cups)
3 to 4 tablespoons milk

1. In large bowl beat shortening and butter until light and fluffy; add vanilla.
2. Beat in sugar, 1 cup at a time, alternately with 1 tablespoon milk until light and fluffy.
3. Keep covered with damp cloth until ready to use. Refrigerate in airtight container up to 2 weeks; beat again before using.

Makes 3 cups.

Chocolate Buttercream Frosting

To Buttercream Frosting add 3 ounces (3 squares) unsweetened chocolate, melted and cooled. Beat until well blended. Or add ½ cup very thick chocolate sauce or purchased chocolate syrup. Beat until well blended.

Orange Buttercream Frosting

Use Buttercream Frosting recipe but omit vanilla and milk and add 1 teaspoon freshly grated orange peel and ¼ cup fresh orange juice. Beat until well blended.

Index, by category

INDEX

INDEX

FOR THE BEST IN PAPERBACKS, LOOK FOR THE

In every corner of the world, on every subject under the sun, Penguin represents quality and variety—the very best in publishing today.

For complete information about books available from Penguin—including Pelicans, Puffins, Peregrines, and Penguin Classics—and how to order them, write to us at the appropriate address below. Please note that for copyright reasons the selection of books varies from country to country.

In the United Kingdom: For a complete list of books available from Penguin in the U.K., please write to *Dept E.P., Penguin Books Ltd, Harmondsworth, Middlesex, UB7 0DA.*

In the United States: For a complete list of books available from Penguin in the U.S., please write to *Dept BA, Penguin,* Box 120, Bergenfield, New Jersey 07621-0120.

In Canada: For a complete list of books available from Penguin in Canada, please write to *Penguin Books Ltd, 2801 John Street, Markham, Ontario L3R 1B4.*

In Australia: For a complete list of books available from Penguin in Australia, please write to the *Marketing Department, Penguin Books Ltd, P.O. Box 257, Ringwood, Victoria 3134.*

In New Zealand: For a complete list of books available from Penguin in New Zealand, please write to the *Marketing Department, Penguin Books (NZ) Ltd, Private Bag, Takapuna, Auckland 9.*

In India: For a complete list of books available from Penguin, please write to *Penguin Overseas Ltd, 706 Eros Apartments, 56 Nehru Place, New Delhi, 110019.*

In Holland: For a complete list of books available from Penguin in Holland, please write to *Penguin Books Nederland B.V., Postbus 195, NL-1380AD Weesp, Netherlands.*

In Germany: For a complete list of books available from Penguin, please write to *Penguin Books Ltd, Friedrichstrasse 10-12, D-6000 Frankfurt Main I, Federal Republic of Germany.*

In Spain: For a complete list of books available from Penguin in Spain, please write to *Longman, Penguin España, Calle San Nicolas 15, E-28013 Madrid, Spain.*

In Japan: For a complete list of books available from Penguin in Japan, please write to *Longman Penguin Japan Co Ltd, Yamaguchi Building, 2-12-9 Kanda Jimbocho, Chiyoda-Ku, Tokyo 101, Japan.*